I'M NOT AFRAID
OF SPIDERS

POEMS ABOUT FEELINGS

JANE ROGERS

For Summer, George and Sophie.

Thanks to Scribbleline for his wonderful illustrations.

Contents

Contents

WHAT ARE FEELINGS?

What are feelings?
Where are feelings?
What do feelings do?
Everyone has feelings
Even me and you.
Happy, Sad, Cheerful, Mad,
Jealous, Bold and Sure.
Loving, Kind, Keen and Eager
Can you think of anymore?

APPREHENSIVE

There are butterflies in my tummy,
And my legs are feeling like jelly.
The water looks inviting
But...
What if I flop on my belly?

They say it's as easy as 123
Diving into a pool,
But I'm not sure I agree.
What if I look a fool?

What do I do with my legs?
How do I hold my arms?
Now I'm starting to shake.
I wish I could stay calm.

Maybe I'll just walk away
I could come back another day.
But...
If I don't try I'll never know
Perhaps I should give it a go.

I'm feeling apprehensive
I don't know what to do.
Shall I be brave and face my fear?
What do you think.
Would you?

HAPPINESS

Happiness is in the sky,
Chasing rainbows, feeling free.
Happiness is when my dog does crazy running
Round and round the tree.

Happiness is lazing in a hammock on a hot summers day,
Bees buzzing, a peaceful dream.
Happiness is hot chocolate
With marshmallows and cream.

Happiness is the smell of coal, waiting at the station.
The whoosh and hiss of an old steam train.
Happiness is jumping on shadows
And dancing in the rain.

THE SEA

'I can see the sea, I can see the sea,
I saw it first, I did, I did!
Stop, stop, I want to get out.'

'Alright' said Dad 'Don't shout,
We have to find a parking space.
Get back in your seat it's not a race.'

'Right now, let's unload the car,
Don't run off, I need to know where you are.
I said DON'T run off come back here.
Listen to me when I say stay near.'

Mum says: 'Hold my hand, we will go together.'
(I'm not doing that, she'll take forever)

Running, running, running, running as fast as I can.
Jumping, skipping, leaping, over the golden sand.
'I can see the sea, I can see the sea,
I'm nearly there, I know I am.'
'I'll swim like a fish
I'll dive like a dolphin,
I'll float on the waves, I know I can.'

'He's faster than a cheetah.'
'Blimey, look at him go.'
'Better catch up with him 'said Mum.
'Alright' said Dad 'I know.'

Running into the water
'Help, it's cold!' Run out.
It makes me laugh, it makes me shiver
'Come on Dad' I shout.

Far up high, floating on the wind,
A seagull watches me.
Dipping and diving over the waves,
Wild and strong and free.

Continued on next page

Time to catch a crab now.
'There's one, there he goes!'
'Pick him up, be careful now
Mind he doesn't pinch your nose.'

Later, on the journey home
Mum says 'Did you like that then?'
'Yes' I say in a sleepy voice.
'When can we go again?'

Let's talk about it

How can you tell what the boy in this poem is feeling?

Why is he so excited?

If you are reading this book with someone else, take turns to talk about the last time you felt excited about something.

If you are reading on your own, have a think about the last time you felt excited, maybe close your eyes while you remember it.

I FEEL FINE

I Feel fine when I'm getting ready for bed.
I wonder what dreams I will dream
In the long night ahead.
I feel fine as I settle down for the night,
Wrapped up in the dark like a bat in a cave,
Until the morning light comes peeping in
At my window.

I feel fine when I'm drawing a picture.
I like to watch it appear on the page.
I might use some colour, or leave it plain.
Sometimes I make a mistake,
And then I have to start all over again.
But I don't mind.
When I'm drawing I feel fine.

I feel fine when I'm picking blackberries.
The plump juicy ones taste best.
I put some in my mouth,
And some in the pot.
Walking home at the end of the day,
I feel fine when I eat the lot!

SAD

Sad is my Dad on a plane
That's a dot in the sky.
Sad is wanting him back
While waving goodbye.
Sad is my smile as I turn away,
And Sad are my tears
At the end of the day.

Let's talk about it

Everyone feels sad sometimes.

Think of a time when you have felt sad.

What made you feel that way?

Can you think of any other words to describe how you feel when you are sad?

FLYING

'Don't get overexcited' said Mum.
'Don't worry, I'm just having fun.'
'Stop that, you're getting too hyper' said Dad.
'Don't worry, I won't do anything bad.'

Arms out stretched
A smile on my face,
I'm flying my plane
We're in a race.

Zooming round the house
Flying up the stairs,
Loop the loop in the kitchen
Jumping off the chairs.

Out into the garden,
'Thank goodness for that' said Mum.
'Oh no, I spoke too soon
Look out here he comes!'

Round and round the sitting room
Faster and faster I go.
Uh oh.... I'm feeling dizzy,
'Look out!'
CRASH!!
'Oh no!'

Now I'm lying on the floor
My head hurts and I'm crying.
'What an earth did you think you were doing?' said Dad.

'I was only flying.'

Let's talk about it

Imagine you are going in a plane tomorrow and you know the pilot will do a loop the loop.

What will you feel like when you are high up in the sky flying in a big circle?

What do you think the boy feels like at the end of this poem?

Use this space to draw a picture of a plane doing a loop the loop.

FEELINGS

What makes you feel happy,

What makes you feel sad.

What makes you giggle,

What makes you mad

Is it OK to feel this way.

What do you do when you're feeling blue,

Do you shout and stamp,

Or run and hide.

What can you do when you're mixed up inside?

Let's talk about it

This poem asks a lot of questions doesn't it.

See if you can answer them.

If you are sharing this book with somebody else you could both take turns to answer.

FRIENDS

My friend was horrid to me today,
When she saw me she ran away.
She told the others not to play,
My friend was horrid to me today.

Let's talk about it

What do you think the girl in this poem is feeling?

If you saw this happening to someone what would you do?

What do you think makes someone a good friend? Make a list here:

PEACEFUL

Peaceful is walking by the seashore
Watching seagulls fly.
Peaceful is lying in the grass
Under the blue blue sky.

Peaceful is the tinkle of cutlery
Being put away in the drawer.
Peaceful is quiet voices talking
In the room next door.

Peaceful is the hush in the church
As the choir begins to sing.
Peaceful is the gentle flutter
Of a butterfly's wing.

Let's talk about it

What does it mean to feel peaceful?

Close your eyes and think of the times when you felt peaceful.

What are you doing?

GOODBYE RABBIT

I'm feeling sad, I don't know why
A tear drop glistens in my eye.
The sky is grey
And I feel blue
I think I might be missing you.

THE DAY SOMETHING GOT BROKEN

'Who broke that?' said Dad as he came in the door
And saw the broken thing lying on the floor.

'He did' my sister said immediately
Pointing an accusing finger at me.

'I didn't touch it' I stammered and stuttered.
'Yes, he did' my sister muttered.

'Well let's say you both broke it' said Dad.
'What do you propose to do?
You can't exactly stick it back together
CAN YOU!

When Mum saw the broken thing, she said:
'Oh, never mind, I didn't like it anyway.'
She's like that, sort of kind.

'Don't worry about Dad' she said.
He's had a tiring day.
Just give him time to calm down.
And clear that broken thing away.'

I'M A BIT WORRIED ABOUT GOING TO SCHOOL

I'm a bit worried about going to school today.
What if I'm asked a question
And I don't know what to say?
Two and two is four,
Three and three is six.
What if the sums are harder than that?
Then I'll be in a fix.

And what if I don't like my lunch?
What if they give me peas?
Will I be too shy to say:
'Can I leave some please?'
What if I can't find a friend when it's time to go out to play?
And what if I get teased Mum?
Oh, PLEASE Mum let me stay.

I'm a bit worried about going to school today,
I'd much rather stay at home.
I don't mind if you have to go to work Mum
I'll be fine all on my own.

Let's talk about it

Most people have something that they worry about from time to time.

Is there anything you worry about?

When you have a worry it's a good idea to talk to someone you trust about it.

Who would you talk to?

Imagine you are friends with the person in this poem.

What do you think you could do or say to make her feel less worried?

BORING SHOE SHOPPING

'Shoe shopping's BORING
Do I really have to come?
These will do for now.'
'No, they won't' said Mum.

'Look I've found a pair I like
Let's order them online.
It's quicker than going into town Mum,
We haven't got the time.'

'Yes, we have and we're going now.
Don't make such a fuss,
Get your coat on hurry up
Or we'll miss the bus.'

'But shoe shopping's BORING
I want to stay at home.'
'Do as you're told and stop moaning,
I'm NOT going on my own.'

'Oh alright, if you insist.
But it will be a waste of time.
I don't want new shoes.
I like these
THEY ARE FINE!'

Let's talk about it

Everyone has to do something they don't want to sometimes.

When do you have to do something you don't like?

How does it make you feel?

If I was with you how would I know what you were feeling?

THE DENTIST'S CHAIR

I like going to the dentist
It has this really cool chair in the room.
I lie back and shut my eyes,
Then I'm flying to the moon.

WHOOSHING round great planets
ZOOMING past the sun,
I'm on an epic journey.
It's only just begun.

Far across the universe
Past the twinkling stars.
Faster than the speed of light
All the way to Mars.
I'm seeing whole new worlds
That no one would believe.
Making friends with aliens.
I never want to leave.

'All done now' the dentist says.
I open my eyes.
Then I'm back in the room.
It's time to leave my rocket chair,
'Please, can I come back soon?'

GRUMPY

'Mum, stop nagging.
You're making me feel grumpy,
I know I need to tidy my room.
Don't go on, I heard you first time
YES, I will do it soon.'

'When?'

'Soon, I promise,
Just let me finish this game.
Don't keep repeating over and over,
You always sound the same.

YES, I know I've got to do my homework.
YES, I will do it very soon.
Now just STOP nagging and leave me alone,
And please get out of my room.'

THE SWIMMING POOL SLIDE

Mum took me to the swimming pool today.
She said 'Do you want to go down the slide?'
'Yes please' I said.
But when I saw it, I thought it looked rather high.

We waited for ages in the queue,
But half way up I needed the loo.
'Oh dear' said Mum. 'What a shame,
I don't think we will get our place again.'

But when we got back the queue had gone.
'That's good' said Mum. 'Come on.'
'Wait Mum I'm scared, I've changed my mind.'
'Oh, don't worry, I'm sure you'll be fine.'

'Sit down, I'll give you a push.'
And off I slid with a great big WHOOSH!
Faster and faster, down and down,
Slipping and sliding, round and round.

Into the pool with a great big SPLASH!
I'm under the water, then up in a flash.
'I'm so proud of you' said Mum
'WOW!' I said 'THAT WAS FUN'

Let's talk about it

Sometimes trying something new can be exciting, but scary as well.

The girl in this poem feels nervous when she sees how big the slide is.

What do you think she is worried about?

How do you think she feels at the end of the poem?

Have you ever had a go at something that made you nervous?

I FELT A BIT EMBARRASSED

I felt a bit embarrassed when my tooth fell out on the bus.
The lady sitting next to me made such an awful fuss.

'Oh, what a lot of blood!' she cried,
'You do look such a sight.'

'Here you are, have my hankie,
Are you sure you are alright?'

'Shall I ask the bus to stop?
Shall I call your Mummy?'

'No, I'm quite ok' I said,
It really wasn't funny.

'Please, don't make such a fuss' I said
'I'm really quite alright.'

'I'm sorry' said the lady
'But you gave me such a fright.'

'You see I'm quite afraid of blood
It makes me feel quite queasy.'

'I'm feeling rather wobbly now,
This really isn't easy.'

'I can't help the blood!' I said,
'Why don't you move your seat?'

But answer came there none
For she had fainted at my feet.

Let's talk about it

Why do you think the boy in this poem felt embarrassed?

I sometimes feel embarrassed if somebody explains to me how to do something, but I still don't understand it. I feel that I will be a nuisance if I have to ask them to explain it again.

Have you ever felt embarrassed about something?

What was it like? If you are reading this book with someone tell them about it, or write about it here:

TRYING TO LEARN

I'm trying to learn to ride my bike,
Wibble wobble wibble wobble.
I'm trying to learn to swim a width
Splash, glug, bubble.
I want to learn to climb a tree
Slip, bump
OUCH MY KNEE!
I'd like to get my spellings right
And have my story read in class.
And when it's time for sports day
I hope I don't come last.

CHRISTMAS MORNING

'It's Christmas day it's Christmas day
Let's see what Santa's brought us!'

'Alright but don't be so loud,
Remember what Mum and Dad told us.'

'Look some Star Wars Lego,
LOOK SOME LEGO I SAID!'

'Ok Ok I heard you first time
Stop jumping on the bed.'

'A spud gun a Yo Yo some chocolate mice,
AND A TOY STORY BOOK!'

I've got LOADS of cool things,
Quick come here and look.'

'WHAT'S GOING ON IN THERE SO EARLY?!'

'It's alright Dad it's nearly light.'

'No it's not look at the clock!
IT'S THE MIDDLE OF THE NIGHT!'

'I don't want to go back to bed,
Can't we play with our toys?'

'Oh, alright if you must,
But remember NO MORE NOISE!'

NOW THAT GRANDAD'S GONE

The day has got a hole in it.
The hole is where you used to be.
I don't know how to fill the hole
Now it's only me.

Let's talk about it

It can be very hard for us when someone or something we love isn't there anymore.
This boy feels as if there is a hole where his Grandad used to be.

Perhaps in time he will be able to fill that hole with happy memories of the good times they had.

What do you think?

I'M FEELING BAD

I'm feeling bad
I'm feeling mad
I'm feeling sad and lonely.
I'm feeling hurt
I'm feeling stressed
I'm feeling that if only
I could bottle up my feelings
And throw them out to sea,
Then I could stand and watch
As they float away from me.

Let's talk about it

We all have difficult feelings sometimes. Wouldn't it be nice if we could just put them in a bottle and throw them out to sea?

Do you have any feelings you would like to watch float away?

If you have any feelings you would like to wave goodbye to write them down here:

I'M CURIOUS

I'm curious to know where the sun goes at night
As I watch it sink down in the sky.
Sometimes it glows like a giant red ball
And I can't help but wonder why.

Why are we here on this planet called Earth?
Does time really fly?
Are angels real or imagined?
And where do we go when we die?

JUST STAY CALM

I had to go to the doctor today
To have an injection in my arm.
I was worried it would hurt.
Mum said: 'Just stay calm.'

It took a lot of courage
To walk into that room.
The doctor smiled at me and said
'It will all be over soon.'

'Now roll your sleeve up young man
I promise to be quick,
Roll it up as far as you can
You may feel a tiny prick.'

The needle looked so sharp
As it came towards my arm.
'Don't look' said Mum 'You're doing fine,
Remember just stay calm.'

I'm feeling faint
I'm feeling sick, I want to shout out 'NO!'
Then Mum says
'Well done, you were so brave,
Now it's time to go.'

I DON'T LIKE THE DARK

I don't like the dark, because when I'm in bed
Scary thoughts come into my head.

I'm in a huge forest far from home,
I'm worried, I'm frightened, I'm lost and alone.

The wolves begin to howl and the vampires to creep,
Scary thoughts in my head keep me from sleep.

I try to think of something nice,
But my brain feels like a stone.
And then the zombies in my head
All begin to moan.

Let's talk about it

Some people love the dark, and some people hate it. How do you feel about the dark?

Use this space to draw a picture from this poem

ANGRY

My sister and my brother were fighting on the floor,
She wacked him with a cushion,
'Help!' he cried 'No more.'
She wacked him with another,
This time round the head.
'Right that's it I'm getting you'
My little brother said.

'You've made VERY ANGRY
I'll get my own back soon.'
And up he got and chased her
Round and round the room.

'HELP, HELP I DON'T WANT TO DIE!'
My sister shouted out.

Then Mum came in and said
'What's all this about?'

'She hit me.'
'No, I didn't let me have my say,
Mum it was an accident
His head got in the way.'

I'M PROUD OF MYSELF

I'm proud of myself
I've learnt something new.
It's not been easy,
It's quite hard to do.
Mum said:
'You won't get good at that overnight.'
'Yes I will' I said
But she was right.
Sometimes I've felt like crying,
But I don't let that stop me from trying.
I tell myself every day
'Don't let anything stand in your way.'
I'm proud of myself for aiming high,
Who knows what else I can do If I try?

Let's talk about it

What does it mean to be proud?

I learnt to ride a horse when I was eight years old, it wasn't always easy, and I fell off quite a few times, but I'm proud that I did it.

Have you done anything that made you feel proud?

Use this space to write about it or draw a picture if you like.

THE WAY I FEEL ABOUT HOMEWORK

'Homework is bad
It makes me mad
I'm not doing it
NO I WON'T.
I'm going to throw it in the bin,
Just you see if I don't!'

'I love doing homework,
I don't care if it takes me all day.
I like to spend ages getting it right,
In my own particular way.'

'I like marking homework.
I like to see what my pupils have done.
But sometimes it takes me all night,
Then it's not quite so much fun.'

Let's talk about it

Do you have to do homework?

How do you feel about it?

If you are someone who likes homework, what is it that you like about it?

If you don't like homework, why is that?

Do you think children should have to do homework?

SNEAKY

Sneaky is the little brother
Who has a cunning plan.

He tip toes gently across the garden,
A jug of water in his hand.
He's heading towards his sister
Who lies sleeping on the ground.
Stealthy like a lion,
He prowls...
Making no sound.

Then suddenly,
Angry shouts and screams
Disturb the peaceful day,
And wicked laughter fills the air
As the little brother runs away.

SOMETIMES I FEEL SHY

Sometimes I feel shy
And I don't know what to say.
The words just won't come out
And I have to turn away.

Sometimes Shy takes hold of me
When there's someone new to meet,
Shy makes me feel quite awkward
So I just stare at my feet.

Sometimes Shy stops me doing things
That other people do,
Like having fun
And making friends
Or trying something new.

'Don't be shy' I tell myself
Nearly every single day.
It never makes a difference though.
Shy is here to stay.

DON'T BE GLUM

'I wish the sun would come out,
It's no fun camping in the rain.
I never, ever EVER want to do this again!'

'My sleeping bag's all soggy, my feet are frozen cold,
They say: 'Everyone should go camping before they get too old.'

But I just don't agree with that
Holidays should be fun,
Building castles at the beach,
Lazing in the sun.'

'Come on' says Dad 'Don't be glum.
It's only a spot of rain,
Don't let it spoil our holiday,
That would be a shame.'

'Take a look outside the tent,
The clouds are on the run,
The breeze has blown them all away.
Come on everyone!'

Racing into the water
Laughing in the sun,
Swimming like a dolphin,
I knew this would be fun!

Who cares about a spot of rain
Or a tiny bit of cold.
Everyone should go camping
Before they get too old.

MY WORRY BOT

I have a little Worry Bot
Who lives inside my head.
He pops up several times a day and says:
'I wouldn't do that,
Is it safe?
What if something bad happens?'
And if I want to try something new
His advice?
'I wouldn't if I were you.'

'Don't read your poem in front of the class
Everyone might laugh.
And best not to go out alone,
You might get lost and never come home.'

'And definitely don't try to make new friends
Anywhere you go,
Some people are not very nice
And you wouldn't even know.'

His busiest time is in the night,
When he goes through my worries one by one.
It keeps me awake but it's important work
I know it's got to be done.

Some people say:
'You worry too much'
And I fear this may be true.
So, I'm going to ask my Worry Bot
What he thinks I should do.

I think that's a good idea.
Do you?

I FEEL A FOOL

I don't like it when I get told off at school,
The other kids laugh and I feel a fool.

I don't like it when people bully me,
I wish they would just leave me be.

I don't like it when I go out to play,
And then get told to 'Go away.'

I'm always pushed to the back of the queue,
I don't like that, would you?

Let's talk about it

I feel sorry for the boy in this poem, do you?

If you were friends with him what advice would you give?

I FELT SCARED IN THE NIGHT

I felt scared in the night
So I called my Dad.
'What's the matter?' he said.

'I don't like the dark
I heard something move,
There's a monster under my bed.'

'There won't be anything there you know,
But I'll take a quick look if you like.
Yep, I was right some toys and some books,
Not a single monster in sight.'

'Please don't leave me alone Dad
I get so scared on my own!'
'Alright I'll sit here till you fall asleep,
No chatting mind, not a peep.'

'The things I do for you kids
It's giving me more grey hairs.
I was in the middle of a really good film,
Before you called me upstairs!'

'What was the film about Dad?
Was there anyone famous in it?
Was it long or short Dad?
Oooh, Dad I've just had a thought...'
'For GOODNESS SAKE SHUSH, now go to sleep,
Remember I said:
NOT a peep.'

'Oh, alright Dad, sorry Dad,
But please don't go away.'

'Just settle down now,
Close your eyes,
And yes...
I promise I will stay.'

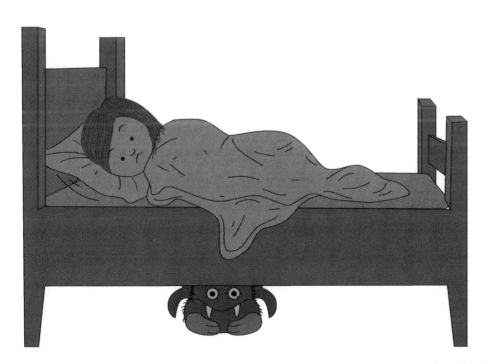

POCKET MONEY FRUSTRATION

'Can I have my pocket money?'
'Of course not it's not due.'

'But Mum, I REALLY need it.'
'Now you know that isn't true.'

'It is there's something I REALLY want
I just can't live without it.'

'Tell me what it is then,
Perhaps we'll talk about it.'

'Oh, what's the point?
You'll just say no
Like you always do.'

'Umm, I see your problem,
That just might be true.'

'Oh, PLEASE MUM let me have it,
I promise I won't ask for more.'

'But that's what you said last week.
And the week before.'

'It's not fair, I'm going out
I don't like you anymore!'

'Alright, I'll see you later.
And please don't slam the door.

Let's talk about it

Isn't it frustrating when you can't have something you really want?

Can you think of anything that makes you feel frustrated?

What do you do when you feel like this?

Use this space to draw a picture of yourself with a grumpy face. Or copy the picture of the boy with the poem.

I LIKE MY STEPDAD

My stepdad is so funny
He always makes me laugh
He picked me up fully dressed
And put me in the bath.

'Stop that messing about you two'
Mum came in and said.
Then my stepdad got my pants
And put them on his head.

HOPING TO HEAR

I've got to have an operation,
There's something wrong with my ears.
The doctor says when it's done
I should be able to hear.

I'm always saying 'What' and 'Pardon'
And 'Can you say that again?'
When I tell my friends: 'I'm not deaf'
They say: 'WASH YOUR EARS OUT THEN!'

It's time to have it done now,
The nurse says: 'Go to sleep.'
I lie back and shut my eyes,
And soon I'm counting sheep.

'Wake up now' I hear a voice
'Everything went well.'
'Has it worked?' I ask.
'I'm not sure if I can tell.'

They said it might be quite a while.
'Lie still and please don't move.'
Oh, I do hope when I get home,
My hearing has improved.

LONELY

I started a new school today,
My 'buddy' asked me out to play.

I said 'If you don't mind
I think I'd rather stay behind.'

I sat in the classroom all alone
A teardrop on my cheek.

My teacher saw.
'Don't worry' she said,
I'll help you through the week.'

PLEASE DON'T

Please don't take me to the bank,

I hate to wait in a queue.

And please don't make me eat vegetables,

It's not a nice thing to do.

Please don't make me go to bed,

Before I want to go.

What's the point of that?

I won't get to sleep you know.

And please don't tell me off

When you think that I've been bad.

I really just can't stand that.

It makes me feel so mad.

CAN YOU IMAGINE

Can you imagine what it feels like
To sleep on the street all alone?
I have no one to love or care for me,
And nowhere to call my home.

Can it be right that some people
Have to live their whole lives in this way?
How I wish I could swap places with you,
Even if just for one day.

Let's talk about it

Sadly, there are some children in this world who don't have a home.

What do you think that's like?

Imagine you are homeless, write about it here or draw a picture.

GUILTY

My brother, my sister and me,

Climbed up into a tree.

My brother fell down and hurt his head,

'You silly little boy!' my sister said.

'Wah Wah Wah'

My little brother cried.

'How did he do that?' said Mum.

'We don't know' my sister lied.

THINGS I LIKE

Snowflakes, angels,
Stars, moon,
Waves, wind,
And dancing kites.
Tigers, horses,
Friends, fun,
Clouds grey and white.
Books, stories, sea, sand,
And dark, dark night.

ANGRY IS THE WAY I DEAL WITH THINGS

Angry is the way I deal with things
When I'm not feeling good.
They say 'Calm down, take deep breathes'.
I only wish I could.
I wish I could control myself
When I get in such a state,
But anger takes control of me
And then it's just too late.

HALLOWEEN

Halloween is coming soon.

We'll go out by the light of the moon.

We'll knock on doors and ask for sweets

From all the houses in our street.

My brother is a scary ghost.

I hope he doesn't get the most!

MAN OF THE MATCH

The coach said
'And now I'm going to announce
Man of the match.'
I looked at my friends,
My friends looked at me.
We all thought the same
Who can it be?

I'd scored a few goals,
But let some in
And Jack and Harry
Had helped our team win.

I looked at the medal
Our coach held up high,
Please let it be me,
Then I caught his eye.
He smiled and winked
As he called my name
'Well done Ben,
You saved the game.'

I'M NOT AFRAID OF SPIDERS

'I'm not afraid of spiders
I'm not scared one little bit.'

'Well then if you're so brave
Why not get closer and touch it?'

'I would if I wanted to
Maybe I don't.'

'You mean you're too scared
That's why you won't.'

'I'm NOT afraid of spiders
'I'm NOT afraid at all.'

'Why are you backing away then?
It's only climbing up the wall.
Look I'm going to pick it up
It's quite friendly really.'

'No don't do that,
I said DON'T do that.
Don't you dare bring it near me.'

'Look at its evil spidery stare,
And feel it's hairy tummy,
Here you are
CATCH!'

'HELP I WANT MY MUMMY.'

Let's talk about it

Lots of people are scared of spiders, and most people have something that makes them feel anxious.

For example:

Dogs

The dark

Getting lost

Snakes

Speaking in front of others

Heights

Flying

Thunder

When I was young I used to be frightened of dolls!

And then one day I won a doll in a raffle. I remember it sitting on the end of my bed, looking at me with it's scary eyes. In the end, I had to ask my Mum to take it away.

Is there anything that you are afraid of or that makes you feel nervous?

What don't you like about it?

Do you think everyone has something they are afraid of?

DON'T MAKE ME MAD

'Go away, leave me alone
I want to play with it on my own.'

'Let ME have a turn or I'll tell Dad.'
'Go away, DON'T make me mad!'

'Give it to me I want a go.'
'Are you deaf?'
I said NO!'

'HEY STOP THAT
Get off, DON'T!'

'YOU IDIOT, now look what you've done!'

'RIGHT THAT'S IT
I'M TELLING MUM!'

Let's talk about it

What does it feel like when someone else has got something you want?

Can you think of a time when this has happened to you?

What might be a solution to this problem?

Use this space to write your ideas:

I'M CURIOUS

I'm curious to know how many times
My heart beats every day.
How did it know when to start?
Was it just made that way?

Why does it sometimes go fast?
And why sometimes ever so slow?
And what keeps it going for all those years?
Does anybody know?

Helping with difficult feelings

We all have difficult feelings sometimes, but what can we do when this happens? Have a go at this next activity, you will need two or more people for this.

- Choose a poem from the list below, and one of you pretend to be the person in the poem. Read the poem out loud, try using your voice to convey the feelings in the poem.

- The people listening need to pretend to be friends with the person reading, and when you have heard the poem ask the reader some questions.

- For example: for 'Apprehensive' you might ask: How well can you swim? Do you feel scared or confident in deep water? How much do you want to be able to dive? What's the best thing that could happen? What's the worst?

- Now try and think together of some ideas and suggestions that might help. Maybe the girl who wants to dive into the pool should watch someone else doing it and try and copy them, what do you think? Or perhaps try the first dive from a sitting position on the edge of the pool? Or what about counting to three then just doing it?

- Think of as many different ideas as you can, discuss them together and see if you can work out what is the best thing to do, take turns being the person to read the poem.

Apprehensive

Sad

Friends

I'm a bit worried about going to school

I don't like the dark

Sometimes I feel shy

My worry bot

Pocket money frustration

Lonely

Angry is the way I deal with things

More activities

- Look at the poem 'My Worry Bot' on page 64
  Draw a picture of the Worry Bot or write a letter to it, what would you say?

- Draw a bunch of balloons, in each balloon write something that makes you feel peaceful, content, happy or excited. See how many balloons you can draw. When you have finished, think about the reasons why these things make you feel this way. Show your picture to someone and talk to them about it.

- Now draw a picture of some clouds, in each cloud write something that makes you feel sad, grumpy, angry or frustrated. Think about why these things make you feel this way. Show your picture to someone and talk about it.

- Start a Feelings Diary.
  Each day write about what has happened and the different feelings that you have had. Illustrate your diary if you like and keep it in a safe place.

- Look at the poem 'I don't like the dark' on page 52
  See if you can re write it from the point of view of someone who loves the dark.

- Imagine you are on the way to school one day and something really unusual or exciting happens. Write about it here, draw a picture to go with your words

- Look at the poem 'Peaceful' on page 26
  Write your own poem about what the word peaceful means to you with each line beginning 'I feel peaceful when........

We're at the end of this book of poems about feelings now, but I feel as if I could go on making up poems about this subject forever.

On the next page you will find a big list of feelings, but there are many more that are not written down here, see if you can think of some.

I think it's quite likely that most of us will at some point in our lives feel nearly every one of those feelings.

That's a lot of feelings!

I'm curious to know what you think of these poems.

If you have enjoyed them please ask your Mum or Dad if they will write a review on Amazon (you can tell them what to say)

That would make me happy!

Thank you

Jane

Some feelings words

Happy	Miserable
Uncertain	Silly
Sleepy	Doubtful
Exhausted	Brave
Overwhelmed	Angry
Intimidated	Irritated
Furious	Amused
Timid	Shy
Energetic	Positive
Delighted	Calm
Tired	Relaxed
Moody	Chilled
Guilty	Nervous
Exhilarated	Stressed
Perturbed	Peaceful
Annoyed	Bored
Greedy	Guilty
Sad	Hopeful
Lonely	Loved

These pages have been left blank for you so you can have a go at writing your own poems about feelings.

Choose from the list of feelings words, or maybe you can think of your own, and don't worry if you find it hard to make up rhymes, poems don't have to rhyme.

Notes for adults

Let's talk about feelings

Being able to talk about feelings and emotions is an important skill for children to develop, and having good healthy emotional intelligence is very valuable, especially when it comes to dealing with difficult feelings in ourselves, or recognising and responding to them in others.

A lot of people, children and adults are not very good at this and some people deal with difficult emotions in unhelpful or unhealthy ways:

Dealing with difficult feelings in unhelpful ways

- Bottling up your feelings, not talking about them.

- Suppressing emotions and trying to forget about them altogether.

- Blaming others for the way we feel.

- Being taken over by difficult feelings, becoming angry and losing control. This is often called acting out.

On the other hand, there are people who deal with difficult feelings and emotions in much more helpful ways. These are people who have good emotional literacy or 'intelligence' and when they experience a difficult or distressing feeling they are likely to go through this process:

Dealing with difficult feelings in helpful ways.

- Recognise the emotion.

- Name it and be able to talk about how they feel.

- Accept difficult feelings without being overwhelmed by them.

- Begin to resolve and problem solve.

- Seek support if they need to.

Clearly the second way of dealing with things when you are experiencing big or difficult emotions is healthier than the first, but of course it takes time for children to learn to respond like this, and of course some children are more emotional than others.

Supporting your child to talk about and deal with their feelings is an important part of parenting.

It can be easier with some children than with others, just as some adults don't like to talk about how they feel, some children are naturally this way inclined too. There are lots of things you can do to encourage your child to express their feelings and the younger you start the better.

Here are some ideas:

Label emotions

This involves naming the emotion as your child has it.

If they are excited about something, point out that that is what they are feeling 'I can see you are feeling very excited about the party today.'

If they are upset about something, name that emotion for them 'It's upsetting when you lose the game.'

Use more advanced feelings word too, remember you want your child to develop a good bank of words they can call on to describe how they feel:

'Are you feeling anxious about moving into a new class? 'You seem agitated, is something bothering you?'

Read books together

Children's books are a wonderful resource when it comes to teaching emotions.

When you are reading with your child don't forget to stop every now and then or maybe when you get to the end of the story, and chat about the feelings and emotions of the characters in the story.

Get your child to tell you how the characters are feeling and ask them if they can think of a time when they have felt the same.

For young children:

If Little Bear is scared of the dark, what does it mean to be scared? What scares your child? What scares you? What can you do if you feel scared about something? Can you think of another word for scared?

Older children:

If your child has got to the stage where they are reading by themselves you can still talk to them about what they are reading, and what the characters are thinking and feeling.

Use films and TV in this way too.

These kind of conversations are so valuable when it comes to emotions talk.

Play feelings charades.

Grab a pen and write a big list of feelings on some paper. Don't be afraid to include words that your child may not understand yet. Cut the words out and put a number on the back of each, then lay face down in front of the players. Players take it in turns to throw a dice, and pick up the ticket with that number on. Read the feelings word on it and mime the feeling. This game is lots of fun especially for those children who like a bit of play acting.

Keep a Feelings diary

Older children often love the idea of writing in a diary. A diary can be used to record things that have happened during the day, and adding 'How it made me feel' at the end can encourage your child to give a voice to their feelings, either in writing or perhaps in pictures. Get some stickers of faces showing different emotions for your child to use and again make sure you encourage them to write about positive feelings as well as the more difficult ones.

And finally…

Be a role model.

How often do you talk about how your own feelings in front of your children?

Children learn by watching and absorbing what you do, so if you want them to learn to talk openly about their feelings, let them see you do it.

Tell your child how you feel about things, keep it on a level appropriate with their age and understanding:

'I felt really **happy** today when I was out in the sunshine'

'I found that newspaper story about….. (beached whales, sick child, lost dog) really **upsetting**.'

'I feel so **frustrated** when I can't find my keys.'

I feel nice and **relaxed** when I'm listening to my favourite music.'

'It made me feel so **annoyed and cross** when the bus was late.'

'I think I'm feeling **anxious** about my job interview tomorrow'

In this way you can introduce 'feelings' words into your daily conversations, which will help your child to do the same.

If you have enjoyed reading this book and found it useful, I would be very grateful if you would take a few minutes to write a review on Amazon.

Many Thanks,

Jane

Books for adults

When I'm not busy writing poems for children I work as a Parent Coach and have written two short parenting books also available on Amazon.

42184436R00060

Printed in Poland
by Amazon Fulfillment
Poland Sp. z o.o., Wrocław